GALILEO GALILEI –
A SHORT BIOGRAPHY

By Doug West, Ph.D.

Galileo Galilei – A Short Biography

Copyright © 2015 Doug West

TABLE OF CONTENTS

PREFACE

Welcome to the book "Galileo Galilei - A Short Biography." This book is part of the "30 Minute Book Series" and as the name of the series implies, if you are an average reader this book will take around 30 minutes to read or a little longer to listen to in audio format. Since this book is not meant to be an all-encompassing, thick biography on Galileo Galilei, you may want to know more about this fascinating man. To help you with this there are several good references at the end of this book. Thank you for purchasing this book and I hope you enjoy your time with Galileo Galilei.

Doug West

July 2015

INTRODUCTION

In Galileo's world, the Sun and all heavily bodies rotated around the Earth. This was the view of the ancient philosopher Aristotle and was widely accepted. His time was a period of religious upheaval as the Catholic Church was in crisis over the Protestant Reformation, which had sown the seeds of discord within the Church. Those thought guilty of heresy were subject to a court of Inquisition, and the consequences could be quite severe if one was found guilty. Galileo was a bold thinker in a time when religion and science merged — new views of the cosmos were not taken lightly. Galileo was a good Catholic and believed that the world was created and controlled by an all-powerful God, but he didn't believe that the Bible should be taken too literally when it came to explaining natural phenomena, such as the motion of the planets through the heavens.

Galileo's works were banned by the Church for centuries and it wasn't until the twentieth century that the rift between Galileo and the Church would be closed. Galileo's work forms the basis of the modern physical sciences and he was one of the key players in the scientific revolution that would change mankind's understanding of the world forever. Not only was he the father of modern science, he had a very practical side as an inventor. He turned what was a mere parlor toy, the spyglass, into a working telescope that was useful to study the heavens and was of practical use to mariners at sea. In addition to the telescope, he made improvements to the microscope, thermometers, clocks, and water pumps. Take the journey into the life of this man who was clearly ahead of his time.

CHAPTER 1 - EARLY YEARS

Galileo was born in February 15, 1564 in Italy when Pisa was part of the Grand Duchy of Tuscany ruled by the House of Medici. Galileo's father was the music theorist, composer, and lutenist Vincenzo Galilei, who was famous for his musical prowess, while his mother was Giulia Ammannati. The Galilei family was of the Italian nobility, but they were not very affluent. Galileo was the eldest of a brood of six or seven children. He was named after Galileo Bonaiuti, an ancestor who lived in Florence in the 14th century. Galileo and his brother Michelangelo took after their father and became accomplished lutenists themselves. The Galilei children were raised pious Roman Catholics, and when he was young Galileo considered entering religious life as a priest.

During his mid-teen years, Galileo was educated at Vallombrosa at the Camaldolese Monastery where he learned about logic and the language of the Greeks, and read extensively on the best Latin authors of this time. His intellect and aptitude for invention were evident at a very young age, as he created toy-machines for amusement. Galileo was exposed to the scientific method early through his father, who conducted experiments on his own and established a non-linear relationship of the square root of the tension and the pitch of a stretched string.

Galileo was removed by his father from the monastery and in 1581 began to study medicine at the University of Pisa. There he received instruction from Andrea Cesalpino, the renowned botanist and physician. The curriculum was controlled at the University of Pisa by the Catholic Church in Rome. However, it turned out that Galileo was not destined to be a doctor of medicine because he would shift his attention to mathematics and natural philosophy. Galileo believed that mathematics was the language of nature and if one was to truly understand the world then you had to understand mathematics.

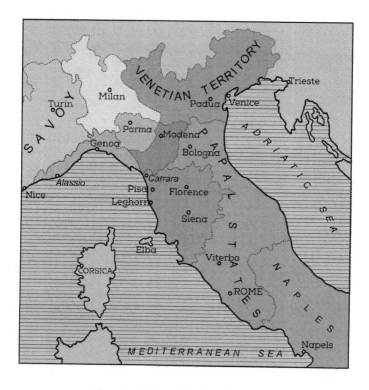

Figure – Map of Italy Circa 1600

While Galileo was a student of medicine in 1581, he attended the Cathedral of Pisa and one day noticed a chandelier that was swinging overhead. He observed that no matter how far it reached, the chandelier took the same time to swing back and forth. He also noted that the chandelier started swinging in a large arc, which became smaller and smaller. His inquisitive mind took to the challenge of the principles behind the behavior of the swinging chandelier. At home, he put up a pair of pendulums of equal length. He swung one with a larger arc, while the other swung at a smaller arc. He discovered that the two pendulums kept perfect time. His observations did not directly result in a practical application, but the incidence awakened in him an interest in mathematics. The property of the constant period of swing of a pendulum would decades later be used as the basis for very accurate pendulum clocks. Eventually, inspired by a lecture on geometry, he persuaded his father to allow him to withdraw from the study of medicine and support his studies in natural philosophy and mathematics. He left the university in 1585 without a degree but continued his studies in mathematics and natural philosophy. He supported himself after he left the university by being a private tutor.

The Aristotelian worldview was the dominant thought at the University of Pisa. It was the leading scientific theory, and more importantly, it was the worldview approved by the Roman Catholic Church. Like his peers, Galileo was initially a staunch supporter of the Aristotelian philosophy, but then as his knowledge grew, he gradually veered away and began to question this ancient wisdom.

In 1588, Galileo unsuccessfully sought a position as an instructor of mathematics at Bologna. Even though he did not win this position, his reputation as a scholar was growing. Later that same year he was asked to deliver two lectures at the Florentine Academy, which was a prestigious literary group. He also developed some ingenious theorems on the centers of gravity which brought him recognition among mathematicians and certain nobleman. In 1589, he did obtain a position teaching mathematics at the University of Pisa. Two years after he began work at the university, his father Vincenzo Galilei died and Galileo became responsible for his younger siblings, which imposed a financial hardship since he only earned a professor's salary.

It was during his time at Padua that Galileo began a relationship with a Venetian woman, Marina Gamba. She became the mother of Galileo's three children, all born out of wedlock. Marina and Galileo didn't live together on a regular basis. She lived in Venice and he lived in Padua where he had a house full of students. The eldest daughter, Virginia, was born in 1600, followed by another daughter, Livia, in 1601, and a son, Vincenzo, in 1606.

Galileo was a studious man of science who followed inductive reason conscientiously, but he also had a social side of his personality. He was an animated, cheerful, and affable man known for generosity and benevolence. He had a quick temper when provoked, but he was not a man to hold grudges. It was known that he offered his home to men of talent who had no financial resources. He was frugal but engaged in the pleasures of the best wines. Because of the pleasures the drink gave him, he cultivated grapevines. Working in his gardens was a great joy for Galileo.

He was also frank in expressing his opinions, but he never imposed intellectual topics on those who were not capable of comprehending the topics he delved into deeply. He sought the gaiety of the company of friends, many of whom favored him. For those who do not share his passion for science, he shared his extensive knowledge of literature. He entertained his social circles with legends and poetry which he could recite from memory. His views were liberal, perhaps too liberal for his time. But this was because of his absolute love for truth. He made plenty of personal sacrifices to arrive at the truth, which he sought with reflection and experimentation. When misfortune befell him later on in life, he continued to show zeal and his stance remained uncompromising.

Chapter 2 - Early Interest in Science and Experimentation

In 1589, while serving as the chair of Mathematics at the University of Pisa, Galileo proceeded with experiments, where he dropped various weights from the famous Leaning Tower. Before Galileo, scientists subscribed to the view propagated by Aristotle that objects which are heavier fall at a faster rate than objects that are lighter. Galileo proved by experimentation that this was not the case. Instead, he reasoned that objects fall at the same speed no matter what their shape and weight. In a vacuum, a wrench and a feather would reach the ground at the same time after being released simultaneously.

Figure – Leaning Tower of Pisa

In studying the motion of falling bodies, Galileo discovered that the speed by which a body falls to the ground is not dependent on its weight. Followers of Aristotle maintained that the manner of falling depends on certain qualities of the object, such that, a one pound rock being lighter than a two-pound rock would fall slower. Galileo contented that when released from a given height, objects on earth reach the ground at different times not because of certain innate characteristics of the object but because of the effects of air friction on the object.

In his studies of falling bodies, Galileo concluded that the distance traveled has a direct relationship with the square of the time it takes to fall. The implication of this law is that the speed of fall increases with time. Galileo determined that force causes acceleration, contrary to the belief of Aristotelian followers who argued that force causes speed.

Galileo developed the concept of inertia from his observations of objects in motion. Since force causes acceleration, he maintained that bodies "do not require a cause" to continue moving, which gave rise to the idea of inertia. This principle states that an object in motion stays in motion in the same direction and with the same speed, while an object at rest will remain at rest unless an unbalanced force acts on it. Galileo's concept of inertia served as the basis for the first law of motion formulated by Sir Isaac Newton. He published his results in a small book entitled *On Motion*. Thus, Galileo took the first step to overthrow the preposterous system of unquestioning adhesion to ancient dogma, which had impeded the development of the knowledge of nature for over a thousand years.

Due to his conflicts with the dogma of Aristotle, his contract was not renewed and in 1592, with the help of his friend, Galileo found a position at the University of Padua. At Padua, he taught subjects such as astronomy, mechanics, and geometry. The University of Padua was founded in 1222 and was controlled by civil authority rather than the Church. Padua is a northern city in Italy near the city of Venice, far enough away from the strict control of the Church at Rome. Galileo would teach at Padua until 1610.

CHAPTER 3 - GALILEO'S TELESCOPE

While teaching at the University of Padua, in 1609, Galileo ventured out to Venice to visit a friend who told him about a Dutchman named Johannes Lippershey, who had invented a new optical device that made distant objects appear to be nearer to the observer. Galileo decided to apply his talents to create a similar device. By trial and error he successfully made a working telescope. The "magical toy" he created consisted of a leaden tube, which contained two spectacle glasses and magnified objects three times their normal size. Galileo's spyglass utilized lenses he procured from the shop of a maker of spectacles. It created a huge buzz in Venice and people flocked to see it. The Doge of Venice, Leonardo Deodati, informed Galileo that the senate wanted to possess such an instrument. Galileo readily complied, and received in return a generous salary increase and the prominent position of Professor at Padua. He soon became one of the highest-paid members of the academe.

Galileo's excellent craftsmanship became apparent as his instruments were better than his contemporaries. After the first telescope, which magnified objects three times, he then produced an instrument that magnified objects eight times. He devoted his time and improved methods to make the lenses that would produce a telescope that had 30 times magnifying power. What set Galileo apart from other scientists who endeavored to make their own telescope was his devotion to produce the best possible instrument. Not satisfied with lenses that he could procure in the area, he learned the art of grinding lenses to make more powerful telescopes.

He made significant discoveries in the field of astronomy with the device that he invented, which turned out to be a technically superior version than the Dutch original. With time and practice, only Galileo and his pupils could produce high quality instruments, which were considered better than the ones produced in Amsterdam, Venice, or Paris. Galileo demonstrated his new spyglass to the officers at the Naval Arsenal of Venice and was able to spot ships at sea two hours before they could be seen with the naked eye. He was given a sum of money for his efforts and his contribution to the re-public. The development of the telescope was a mixed blessing for Galileo; on one hand, it increased his prominence and his financial position, and on the other hand, his discoveries with the new telescope would lead to serious trouble in the future.

CHAPTER 4 – ASTRONOMI-
CAL DISCOVERIES

The Moon, Earth's one and only natural satellite, was Galileo's first subject for his investigation of the heavens using the telescope he perfected. By the fall of 1609, he was using a telescope capable of magnifying heavenly objects 20 times. By December of that year, he produced detailed illustrations of the phases of the moon and presented surface characteristics never before observed. Before the telescope, everyone thought that the moon had a smooth surface.

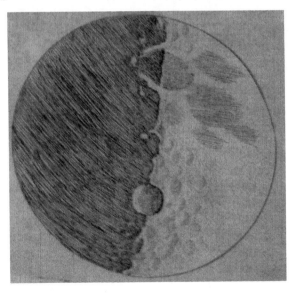

Figure – Galileo's Drawing of the Surface of the Moon

Galileo discovered similarities between the surface features of his home planet and its nearest neighbor. Because he had the instrument to examine the lunar surface in detail, he spent time observing the terrain and mapping the physical features of the lunar disc. Galileo observed summits outlined by the light from the Sun, while at the same time noting hollow areas that were still in shadow. From his observations, Galileo attributed the phosphorescence that observers of the night sky noted during the last and first quarters of Moon to reflected sunlight from the Earth. Meanwhile, he thought that the dark spaces he saw on the surface were continents and seas. After seeing the mountains and valleys of the Moon magnified, he then turned his attention to the fixed stars and the planets of the Solar System. For Galileo, the irregularities he found on the Moon's surface were evidence of "divine wisdom." He argued that a vast, featureless surface would indicate that it was "the abode of silence and inaction—senseless, lifeless, soulless, and stripped of all those ornaments which now render it so varied and so beautiful."

One of the bright "wonderers" of the night sky is Jupiter, which is the fifth planet from the Sun. Before Galileo, the existence of its family of satellites was yet unknown. When Galileo trained his telescope at Jupiter on January 7, 1610, he saw three fixed stars near the planet's body. The stars were brighter than others of similar magnitude. He found them lying parallel to the ecliptic, on the same plane in a straight line, with one "star" located west of him and two located east of him. Galileo dismissed them to be "fixed stars" and did not pay attention to their distances with respect to Jupiter. The next night, when Galileo viewed the "stars" again, the three points of light were closer to each other than they were the night before. Moreover, they were almost equidistant. Galileo's inquisitive mind started pondering the reason for the change in position of the points of light he had observed for two consecutive nights. Galileo kept observing the "fixed stars" and found they continued to shift in position relative to the planet. On the night of the tenth, he attributed the disappearance of one of the points of light to its change in position from the front of Jupiter to its hind part, from the point of view of an observer from Earth. Galileo only saw two stars to the east of Jupiter. His telescope revealed the same situation on the night of the 11th, and yet the easterly star was twice as large as its neighbor. He ruminated on his observations and wrote, "...There were in the heavens three stars which revolved round Jupiter, in the same manner as Venus and Mercury revolve round the sun."

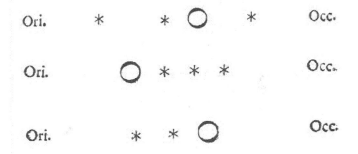

Figure – Galileo's Drawings of the Moons of Jupiter on 7 to 10 January, 1610

Based on the data he collected, he concluded that the three points of light were not fixed stars as he originally surmised, but were in fact the planet's natural satellites. This was a momentous achievement, one of the most important discoveries that will be tied to his name. Galileo had just discovered three of Jupiter's biggest moons. In subsequent observations, he came upon the fourth Jovian moon on January 12. He persisted in observing the four moons revolving around Jupiter until March 22, focusing his efforts on determining their motions. For reference, he used the fixed stars within the field afforded him by the telescope. With continued observations of these heavenly bodies through the middle of 1611, Galileo also came up with estimations of each of the moon's periods, which came very close to modern measurements. The scientific community was at first in doubt that Galileo could make such a breathtaking discovery. But his observations were confirmed soon enough in Christopher Clavius' observatory.

Galileo named the quartet of moons "Medicean Stars," after the family of the Grand Duke of Tuscany, his future patron Cosimo II de' Medici. He dedicated the official account of the discovery in *The Sidereal Messenger*, which he wrote shortly after his observations. The "Medicean Stars" were renamed the Galilean satellites by astronomers who came after their discoverer. Modern students of science know the Galilean moons by their individual names—Callisto, Europa, Ganymede, and Io. It was a revolutionary finding because it did not conform to geocentrism, which dictated that all heavenly beings must revolve around the Earth.

The discovery of the four moons of Jupiter had far reaching implications, namely, that the Earth was not the center of the universe. The response from the geocentric camp was predictable. The loyal followers of Aristotle dismissed Galileo's published work and despite the author's repeated requests to look through his telescope, Padua's principal professor of Philosophy refused to undergo the exercise. The first printing of *The Sidereal Messenger* sold out quickly. At this point in his life, Galileo was not a modest man — he became arrogant about his discoveries. The foremost thinkers chose to adhere to the view that the natural satellites revolving around Jupiter were non-existent. They continued to deny the possibility of centers of motion in the universe other than the Earth.

Meanwhile, when German astronomer and mathematician Johannes Kepler was told of the breakthrough of the Italian from Padua, his contemporary responded with feelings of disbelief and agitation at what he first considered absurd news. He wrote later on that his immediate thoughts, upon parting with the friend who joyfully gave him the news, were that the existence of the additional planets would overturn his work, *Cosmographic Mystery*. Nevertheless, he started thinking about discovering moons orbiting the other known planets.

Perhaps it is not altogether surprising that someone else claimed ownership of the discovery of Jupiter's moons. An astronomer of questionable reputation made a false claim that he discovered the four moons on December 29, 1609, before Galileo. Other astronomers followed suit, claiming to discover more moons. These "moons" were proven to be fixed stars, and the astronomers who made the claims were soon forgotten, as were their baseless discoveries.

Chapter 5 - Move to Florence

Aside from acquiring fame and prominence in the scientific community, Galileo benefited from the discovery of the four largest moons of Jupiter with an increase in his salary. He resigned his professorship at the University of Padua to become the Grand Duke of Tuscany's philosopher and principal mathematician. He was paid the handsome sum of 1000 florins to give lectures to princes. He moved from Padua to Florence, which was the domain of the Medici Family. The Medici family dominated banking and commerce in the region and were also influential in matters of the church. Galileo was encouraged to engage in activities to further his inquiries into the subjects of local motion and mechanics, and to continue his pursuits in determining the nature of the universe. These were all within the scope of his official duties. From then on, Galileo lived a gentleman courtier's lifestyle. Though Galileo's new position was definitely a move up in stature, it also came with some concerns; namely, in Florence beliefs were more influenced by the church than in Padua. For a man with radical beliefs about the order of the Solar System, this would prove to be dangerous.

Leaving behind his mistress in Padua, Galileo placed his two daughters in a convent of San Matteo in Arcetri. This was not an unusual occurrence at the time; daughters born out of wedlock had few prospects for marriage and it was an honor for the family to have children in service to the church.

Both girls would have needed large dowries to find a proper husband and Galileo was not financially able to provide the money necessary for the dowry. Placing the two girls at the convent did not relieve Galileo of the responsibility of their care. He was frequently called upon to provide money, food, and wine to his daughters to help with their support. Life at the convent was a life of poverty and they had want for many things that the convent just could not provide. Nuns during that time became very separate from the outside world and their families and personal visits were minimal; however, Virginia was good about writing her father. Dozens of letters from Virginia to her father have survived, and they give insight into her day-to-day life within the convent walls, as well as the life of her father. Unfortunately, only the letters from Virginia to her father have survived. His letters have been lost to history.

The Earth based model of the solar system had been worked out by the Greek philosopher, Ptolemy. His model had elaborate ways of computing the positions of the planets in the sky. To a person on the Earth there was no physical reason to believe that the Earth was in motion around the Sun. If the Earth were moving then clouds would fly off into the Western sky. The Catholic Church fully endorsed the belief that the Earth was the center of the Solar System, not the Sun. Years before Nicholas Copernicus, a Polish priest and astronomer, had proposed that the Sun, the heliocentric view, and not the Earth, the geocentric view, was the center of the Solar System. Galileo believed that Copernicus was correct but had no way of proving this theory.

The fixed stars and planets have remarkable differences based on Galileo's observations through his telescope. He remarked that the stars presented as lucid points that send out rays that twinkle, whereas the planets were more similar to the moon in that they consistently presented as round globular discs upon magnification.

Figure - The constellation Orion.

Galileo also studied nebulae and found that they appear as a single point of light as seen by the naked eye, but they were actually composed of many different clusters of stars when viewed through the a telescope. He studied the stars in the Praesepe nebula, and the sword and belt of the constellation Orion. In the cluster of The Seven Sisters or Pleiades, Galileo discovered at least 40 individual stars, many more than were visible without the telescope. He also observed that the great Milky Way nebula is composed of a huge number of individual stars.

Galileo also observed the planets Venus and Saturn. He observed the appearance of Saturn, which was puzzling — the planet had something that looked like ears protruding from each side of it. His small telescope was not powerful enough to resolve what we now know are rings around the plant. His observations of Venus were more fruitful. Over the period of several months he observed that Venus went through a series of phases, from a small round disk and then various phases of crescents — much like the Moon. Galileo knew that his observations of the phases of Venus was direct evidence that the Sun was at the center of the Solar System and not the Earth.

Figure – Galileo's drawings of the phases of Venus.

Galileo also observed the Sun and wrote a treatise about sunspots. With his small telescope he developed a method of projecting the Sun's image on a screen where he tracked and recorded sunspots as they moved across the face of the Sun. German Jesuit and Professor Christoph Scheiner also observed sunspots and argued that sunspots were satellites revolving around the Sun. On the other hand, Galileo maintained that they were found near or at the surface of the Sun itself and do not revolve around it like the planets. The controversial debate about this phenomenon, which Galileo discovered independently, was documented in Galileo's *History and Demonstrations Concerning Sunspots and Their Properties.* This book, released in 1613, gave a detailed set of illustrations of how sunspots grow and evolve on the surface of the Sun. The movement of the sunspots across the surface seemed to indicate that the Sun rotated.

CHAPTER 6 - GALILEO THE INVENTOR

Galileo was not just preoccupied with philosophical investigations; he was a very practical man and was involved in the development of new technology. The impetus for his work on devices was partially to satisfy his creative nature and also to provide financial assistance. Over the years, several of his creations were sold at a profit and this provided needed income.

In 1593, Galileo invented a forerunner to the modern thermometer — a device known as a thermoscope. The instrument consisted of a tube and air bulb ensemble. The temperature readings are revealed by the contraction and expansion of air, which then moves the water level in the tube. Galileo's investigations into the nature of why some objects float in water and other objects sink was key to the development of a thermometer that works on the principle of buoyancy. Around 1603, Galileo, his students, and other inventive types developed what is now called the Galileo thermometer. The thermometer is made of a sealed glass cylinder containing a clear liquid and several small sealed vessels of varying densities. As the temperature changes, the individual floats rise or fall in proportion to their density. The float in the center of the thermometer gives the approximate temperature.

In 1596, Galileo published a book which discussed the details of a design for a hydrostatic balance. He had invented the device, and the small book that was published on the topic brought him to the attention of the important scholars of his time.

One of his earliest creations was a geometric and military compass, which was believed to be devised sometime between 1595 and 1598. This instrument was useful to gunners who needed to compute the charge of gunpowder when they used cannonballs of various dimensions. In geometry, the device was an accurate tool for the computation of the area of a polygon, among other calculations. Marc'Antonio Mazzoleni, the prominent instrument maker, produced more than a hundred of Galileo's devices. The compass was sold for 50 lire apiece, and the detailed instructional manual would sell for 120 lire each.

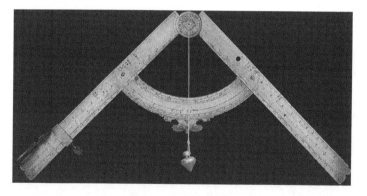

Figure - Galileo's Geometric and Military Compass

Like the telescope, Galileo helped make the compound microscope a more practical and useful device. The credit for the invention of the microscope goes to two Dutch spectacle makers around 1590. By 1609, Galileo had made improvements to the microscope by adding a focusing mechanism. The first comprehensive illustrations of insects were made with one of Galileo's microscopes in 1625.

CHAPTER 7 - ACCUSATIONS OF HERESY

Galileo was vocal in his support of Polish astronomer Nico-laus Copernicus, who proposed that the Sun and not the Earth was at the center of the Solar System. Galileo wrote exten-sively about heliocentrism and he tried to interpret Biblical passages. In his opinion, Biblical texts must not be inter-preted literally, and therefore, the heliocentric point of view was not contrary to Catholic teachings. Meanwhile, most of Europe's educated elite were of the Aristotelian view of a geocentric universe, wherein the Earth was at the center and all the heavenly bodies.

As Galileo's Sun-centered ideas spread throughout Italy, so did opposition to his ideas. He was being publicly denounced from the pulpits by priests and berated by academics. Gali-leo had counted on support of his position from the Medi-ci family, but that was starting to erode. Grand Duchesse Christina worried that Galileo was contradicting the Bible. Galileo answered the Duchesses' concerns in a lengthy letter that went beyond astronomy. The letter would be published many years later in 1636, entitled *Letter to the Grand Duch-ess Christina*. Galileo's contention was that the passages in the Bible that would seem to indicate that the Sun revolved around the Earth were being mis-interpreted and the Bible should not be used as an astronomy textbook. Galileo's let-ter, rather than putting to rest the controversy, merely added fuel to the growing debate — his letter seemed to contradict scripture. The letter was copied and spread thought the religious community and priests were calling for Galileo to be investigated as a heretic.

Being called before the Church's Inquisition was no small matter. They had the power to ban books, imprison a heretic and, if the offence was severe enough, even execution was an option. In 1615, the book published by Paolo Antonio Foscarini, a cleric who wrote that the theory put forward by Copernicus was in no way conflicting with the Holy Scriptures, was banned. Even the book by Johannes Kepler, a non-theological publication of a technical nature entitled, *Epitome of Copernican Astronomy*, was banned by the church. In 1593, the priest Giordano Bruno was called before the Inquisition and sentenced to death and in 1600, he was burnt at the stake in Rome. Bruno was like many others during that period that were found guilty of heresy and sentenced to prison or death. Like Galileo, Bruno believed in the Copernican model and had other far-reaching ideas of the universe. Bruno had many other substantial charges against him that didn't relate to astronomy — such as his disbelief in the divinity of Christ, rejection of the concept of a Trinity, and his belief of the non-virgin birth of Christ. Bruno's fate must have weighed heavily on Galileo as he was being investigated by church officials. The Church wanted to make it very clear that opposing views would not be tolerated and orthodoxy would be enforced. After the German monk, Martin Luther, started the Protestant Reformation in the early 1500s, the Catholic Church had become more ridge in its beliefs and refuted nearly all of Martin Luther's claims against the Church.

Figure - Statue of Giordano Bruno in Rome

In order to defend his ideas, Galileo journeyed to Rome in the winter of 1615. Galileo had not officially been charged with heresy and he wanted to keep it that way. Cardinal Bellarmine was the head of the Inquisition and was the same Cardinal that was responsible for Giordano Bruno being burnt at the stake. Galileo confidently pleaded his case before the group of theologians that the Earth was not the center of the Solar System. The Medici family had an ambassador that attended the hearing and he became concerned that Galileo's brash manners and heretical talk might drag the family into the conflict, as Galileo was an employee of the family. The Church's official findings were that heliocentrism was "foolish and absurd in philosophy, and formally heretical" citing contradictions with the Holy Scripture. Cardinal Bellarmine delivered the findings to Galileo under instruction from Pope Paul V. Galileo was summoned to the Cardinal's residence on the 26th of February, 1616. Galileo was admonished "not to hold, teach, or defend" the Copernican theory "in any way whatever, either orally or in writing." Galileo was forced to refute the ideas of Copernicus and the work of Copernicus was placed on the list of books banned by the church.

CHAPTER 8 – PUBLICATION OF "DIALOGUE"

In 1623, a new Pope took the head of the Catholic Church, his Holiness Urban VIII. Galileo knew this new Pope back when he was a Cardinal. This new Pope was a fan of Galileo and they corresponded with each other. Galileo made the long two week journey to Rome to meet with his old friend. Once at the Vatican, the Pope and Galileo had six separate meetings and ate together. The discussed various topics, one of which was the ideas of Copernicus. Galileo told the Pope about his theory of the tides, which he put forward as a proof of the annual and diurnal motion of the Earth. The Pope told Galileo that he could write about the universe but only treat the Copernican theory from a purely hypothetical perspective.

Emboldened by his conversations with the Pope, Galileo threw himself into writing what would be his masterwork on the cosmos, entitled *Dialogue Concerning the Two Chief World Systems*. The Pope demanded that the publication must present arguments both for and against the Copernican theory. The Pope also requested that the content exclude any direct advocacy for heliocentrism. Galileo was now sixty years old and in poor health. It took him five years to finish his book and he was assisted by his eldest daughter from the convent. Evidence indicates that she prepared the final versions of the manuscript for publication. Galileo finished his great book on Christmas Eve in 1629.

The book is a running dialog debating the two positions, one being that Earth is the center of the universe and the opposite was that the Sun was the center. The dialogue in the book is between a host and his two talkative guests who discuss the two worldviews. The geocentric view was presented through a character who was essentially a simpleton. The words of the Pope were stated through the "Simplicio" character, who argued for geocentrism. Overall, the volume was a strong defense for heliocentrism and an attack on geocentrism. Galileo's approach to cosmology was fundamentally spatial and geometrical: The Earth's axis retains its orientation in space as the Earth circles the Sun, and bodies not under a force retain their velocity. Galileo gave Simplicio the final word, that God could have made the universe anyway he wanted to and still made it appear to us the way it does.

Figure – Galileo Facing the Inquisition

Galileo's book passed the review of the Florentine censor and begun publication in 1630. The next step was for the book to delivered to Rome for final approval so it could be widely distributed. The word from Rome would have to wait — the bubonic plague struck Italy and everyone was quarantined to prevent spread of the contagion. It would be months before Galileo would receive word from Rome on the fate of his book. The book finally reached Rome and the Pope was told that Galileo's work was more literature than a scientific discourse and the Pope was made to play the fool. Pope Urban felt insulted and took a very angry view of the book. This severed the relationship between Galileo and the Pope. The Pope had a panel convened to investigate the book — their recommendation was that it was a matter for the Inquisition and Galileo was ordered to appear before the Inquisition.

In the month of February in 1633, Vincenzo Maculani, the Inquisitor, conducted Galileo's trial. At first, Galileo was adamant that he kept the promise he made not to defend or advocate the concepts the Church declared to be heretical. The Inquisition presented the sentence on June 22. The book he wrote, *Dialogue Concerning the Two Chief World Systems,* was banned. Moreover, any future written work he produced would not be allowed to see print. He was found "vehemently suspect of heresy" by proposing that the Sun, not the Earth, was at the center of the universe, which was contrary to the declarations of the Holy Scripture. The Inquisitor gave Galileo the option to "abjure, curse, and detest" his heretical view; under duress, he complied. The final sentence was imprisonment. At age 70, with poor health, imprisonment in the dungeons of Rome would have been a death sentence. Galileo was able to work out an arrangement with the Church and he was given house arrest.

Chapter 9 – House Arrest and Latter Years

After the trial he initially stayed for a few months with his friend, the Archbishop of Siena, then he returned to his villa in Arcetri, near Florence. In 1634, the sentence was put into effect. Under house arrest, Galileo was not able to teach, travel, or visit his daughters in the convent without permission. Galileo's daughter, Virginia, who had taken the name Sister Maria Celeste in the convent, took it upon herself to read seven penitential psalms once a week for three years, relieving Galileo of the burden imposed by the Inquisition. Galileo was kept under house arrest at his villa in Arcetri, until his death. In 1638, he lost his sight and was allowed to get medical advice in Florence for his insomnia and symptoms of hernia.

Galileo remained productive despite the limitations imposed on his lifestyle by the sentence handed down to him by the Inquisition. Though banned from astronomy, Galileo compiled his earlier works on motion in a book entitled *Two New Sciences*. This work was a compilation of Galileo's studies done some forty years before and completed during the years he was under house arrest. The two main topics covered were kinematics and strength of materials. For the first time, he discussed in detail his interpretations of the parabolic path of projectiles and the law of falling bodies. The book had to be smuggled out of Italy to avoid Church censorship and was published in Holland. This book would form the basis of modern physics and would be instrumental in the work of Isaac Newton just a few years after Galileo's death.

On January 8, 1642, Galileo died after experiencing diffi-
culty with heart palpitations and fever. At his death, he was
surrounded by his son Vincenzio and his disciples, Vincenzio Viviani and Evangelista Torricelli. Because of the verdict
of heresy set before him, Pope Urban VIII was vehemently
against plans to bury him at the Basilica of Santa Croce's
main body, where his father and ancestors were interred.
Instead, Galileo was quietly buried at the Church of Santa
Croce in Florence, in an unmarked grave located in an out-
of-the way room behind the sacristy. In 1737, his remains
were exhumed and buried in an elaborate tomb within the
main body of the Basilica of Santa Croce.

Figure – Galileo's Burial Monument and Tomb at Santa Croce

CHAPTER 10 - SCIENTIFIC LEGACY

According to Albert Einstein, Galileo is the father of modern science and the contemporary cosmologist and theoretical physicist Stephen Hawking said Galileo was responsible for the birth of modern science — far more than anyone else. Today, young students know of Galileo as the father of modern astronomy, as well as a celebrated physicist and mathematician.

Many of Galileo's experiments, observations, and analyses have laid the foundation for key discoveries and inventions accomplished by men and women of science who came after him. However, perhaps his biggest contribution to human civilization is to state and demonstrate that natural laws are mathematical in nature. He was an original thinker and one of the first to uphold this principle. He wrote of nature, "It is written in the language of mathematics, and its characters are triangles, circles, and other geometric figures..." In order to perform the experiments he had in mind, Galileo set standard procedures and methods of measurement, which was a huge leap in human thought. With standards of measure, experiments could be replicated and research studies became reproducible. Moreover, Galileo showed the merits of keeping an open mind and being responsive to the results of experimentation and observation. As a consequence, his contemporaries and the next generation of thinkers found a new appreciation for the relationship between experimentation and theoretical work.

Galileo put the knowledge formulated by scholars before him to good use. From what he learned, he endeavored to separate philosophy and religion from science, which was a major development in thought given the overwhelming influence of Christianity in scholarly studies during his time.

While studying the law of falling bodies, Galileo devised the method of indivisibles, which eventually gave rise to infinitesimal calculus. This pioneering work in Mathematics was not his only contribution to the field; he also utilized mathematical methods as standards tools in experimental physics in innovative ways never before seen.

Modern astronomers named the Asteroid 697 "Galilea" in honor of Galileo. In 2009, the International Year of Astronomy commemorative coin featured Galileo Galilei as a main motif. The coin design was chosen in order to commemorate 400 years of the discovery of the Galilean telescope. In the same year, the consumer market saw the release of the low-cost, high quality, two-inch telescope called "the Galileoscope." Galileo figures repeatedly in popular culture, with his name cropping up repeatedly in songs, plays, and other forms of entertainment.

Figure – Artist's conception of the Galileo Spacecraft investigating Jupiter and Io (photo courtesy NASA)

In 1989, Galileo was honored with the launch of a planetary space probe named after him. Naming the spacecraft after Galileo was very appropriate since Jupiter and its moons were the primary target of the investigation for the spacecraft. The probe Galileo arrived at Jupiter on December 7, 1995, after gravitational assisted flybys from Venus and the Earth. It became the first spacecraft to orbit Jupiter and launch a probe into the atmosphere. Despite suffering mechanical problems, *Galileo* achieved the first asteroid flyby, of 951 Gaspra. The space probe was very successful and transmitted back to

Earth a wealth of valuable scientific information about Jupiter and its moons.

Over the years after Galileo's death, the Church's position on his scientific views softened. As the scientific revolution progressed, the separation between religion and science widened. With Church approval in 1744, a four-volume collection of Galileo's works were published in Padua. In 1835, the *Catholic Index of Prohibited Books* omits from the list Galileo's *Dialogue*, as well as books by Copernicus and Foscarini. The Church fully exonerated Galileo in 1992 when Pope John Paul II conceded that Galileo's trial was not merely an error but also an injustice and that Galileo was theoretically correct about scriptural interpretations.

Photo Credits

All photos are from the public domain unless explicitly noted.

Selected Biography

Finocchiaro, Maurice A. (editor and translator) *The Essential Galileo*. Hackett Publishing company, Inc. 2008.

Hall, John H. (general editor). *History of the World – Earliest Times to the Present Day.* World Publications Group, Inc. 2005.

Heilbron, J.L. *Galileo*. Oxford University Press. 2010.

Sobel, Dava. *Galileo's Daughter: A Historical Memoir of Science, Faith, and Love*. Walker & Company. 2011.

Video: Nova Galileo's Battle for the Heavens (PBS Documentary) by Kristen Cherye. 2002.

About the Author

Doug West is a retired engineer, small business owner, and an experienced non-fiction writer with several books to his credit. His writing interests are general, with expertise in science, history, biographies, numismatics, and "How to" topics. Doug has a B.S. in Physics from the Missouri School of Science and Technology and a Ph.D. in General Engineering from Oklahoma State University. He has also completed additional graduate studies in Astrophysics at Wichita State University. He lives with his wife and little dog "Scrappy" near Kansas City, Missouri. Additional books by Doug West can be found at www.amazon.com/Doug-West/e/B00961P-J8M or on Facebook at www.facebook.com/30minutebooks.

INDEX

A

Arcetri 21, 39
Aristotle 1, 9, 10, 11, 18
astronomy 11, 14, 31, 32, 39, 41

B

Bible 1, 31
Bruno 32, 33

C

Cardinal Bellarmine 33
Catholic Church 1, 4, 5, 22, 32, 35
Compass 28
Copernicus, N. 22, 31, 32, 34, 35, 44

D

Dialogue Concerning the Two Chief World Systems 35, 37

E

Earth 1, 15, 16, 17, 18, 22, 24, 31, 33, 35, 36, 37, 43

G

Galilei, Galileo i, ii, iii, v, 1, 3, 4, 5, 6, 7, 9, 10, 11, 13, 14, 15, 16, 17,
        18, 19, 21, 22, 23, 24, 25, 27, 28, 29, 31, 32, 33, 34, 35, 36,
        37, 39, 40, 41, 42, 43, 44, 46
Galilei, Vincenzo 3, 6, 37
geocentrism 18, 36

V

51336592R00033

Made in the USA
Middletown, DE
01 July 2019